Ready to Teach!

Quick & Easy

Adult Bible Studies to Prepare in Just Minutes

ROBERT L. KITCHEN

STANDARD PUBLISHING

Cincinnati, Ohio

All Scripture quotations, unless otherwise indicated, are taken from the HOLY BIBLE, NEW INTERNATIONAL VERSION®. NIV®. Copyright © 1973, 1978, 1984 by International Bible Society. Used by permission of Zondervan Publishing House. All rights reserved.

Edited and designed by Theresa C. Hayes
Cover by Barry Ridge Graphic Design, photo by SW Productions

The Standard Publishing Company, Cincinnati, Ohio. A division of Standex International Corporation

05   04   03   02   01   00   99   98   5   4   3   2   1

Preface

It has been my experience as a member of several congregations that there are many times when a substitute teacher is needed at the last minute. Due to illness or some other emergency, someone is called on to teach without much time for preparation.

What do you normally do in these situations—panic? Would you like to have access to a series of stand-alone lessons that:
- can be easily prepared in just minutes
- cover a wide variety of situations
- are easy to customize to your needs
- are adaptable to many age groups
- come complete with useful and thought-provoking illustrations
- and contain suggestions for lesson delivery?

You are holding just such a book. These lessons are designed around reproducible handouts that are the focal point of the lesson. These attention-getting handouts provoke thought and discussion that take away the burden of a lecture presentation. Also, each lesson contains a number of questions to help spur discussion. Obviously, the teacher's own methods and practices (including lecture) may be incorporated.

HOW TO USE THIS BOOK

Confucius said, "A picture is worth a thousand words." That's the premise behind this book. Each lesson comes with a handout for you to photocopy and distribute to your students. The handouts are printed two to a page, so you will need to photocopy and cut the pages in half before class time.

EACH HANDOUT IS DESIGNED TO:
- catch the student's attention
- serve as a focal point of the lesson
- be used as a way to follow the lesson's progression
- provide a place to make notes
- provide a visual reminder of the lesson content.

Introduce yourself to the class if necessary and pass out the sheets that you have prepared beforehand. Begin and end each lesson with prayer, if that is your pattern.

The lesson presentation (on the left) may be read verbatim or you may flesh it out, using this material as a guide. Either way, you will be able to assemble a reasonable and useful lesson in short order.

The material on the right is there to prompt your interaction with the class. The answers (provided in italics) are not necessarily the only answers. Your students may come up with other ideas that will increase the depth of the lesson. Make notes of their answers so that pertinent points can be addressed. Replies or comments that seem off base may be brought into focus simply by asking how this answer applies to the illustration. If you have a chalk board or an easel pad, write the comments for all to see. For most lessons, you will want some kind of board to write on.

Here's to a happy substitute teaching experience. With *Ready to Teach!* you need never panic again!

RLK

Something to Grow By

GALATIANS 5:22

TO THE STUDENTS	FOR THE TEACHER
• The graphic on your handout represents our subject today. We're going to start this lesson by finding out what we already know. Please don't look up the Scripture yet, but tell me, what do you see here? What does this rather unusual-looking plant represent?	**Listen for all kinds of answers, including:** *1) Our need to grow* *2) Evidence of growth* *3) Ideas on how to grow*
• For more on the subject of growth, let's look up these verses: Luke 2:52; 1 Peter 2:1, 2; 2 Peter 3:18; 2 Thessalonians 1:3	**List references on the board before class. Ask volunteers to read each verse aloud.**
• What ideas about growth do we get from Luke 2:52? 1 Peter 2:1, 2? 2 Peter 3:18? 2 Thessalonians 1:3?	**Read each verse and discuss.**
• How does the growth process take place in nature? Look at the drawing to see how many steps you can name.	*A plant begins with a seed, sprouts, grows to a plant and bears fruit.*
• What are purposes of roots? Of a stem? Of branches?	*Life line, source of nourishment, support.*
• What are the "roots" in our lives? What provides us with nourishment and support?	*Bible school, worship, group and individual study, prayer, serving others, etc.*

• In nature there are restrictions and obstacles to growth. How many can you name?	**List answers (below) on a board or chart.**	
	Drought	*Lack of study*
	Storms	*Problems*
• Now, can you name some spiritual parallels to these natural problems? What causes us to experience "drought" in our spiritual growth?	*Neglect*	*Not assembling*
	Weeds	*False teaching*
	Insects	*Bad attitudes*

• Galatians 5:19 gives us a list problems that inhibit spiritual growth. What do we find there and what do these words mean?

Encourage answers and list them.

Discord	*lack of harmony, conflict, not getting along*
Dissension	*violent quarreling*
Factions	*cliques, partisan conflict*
Jealousy	*envy, resentment*

• Let's go back to our graphic. What have you filled in? Has anyone named the fruit of the Spirit? Did you get all nine? Let's look them up in Galatians 5:22. Write them down as we read them.

Love, joy, peace, patience, kindness, goodness, faithfulness, gentleness, self-control

• Do you see anything significant in the sequence? Love is first on the list. Some teachers think that the sequence suggests a building process in which the development of each fruit depends on the prior development of the preceding fruit. Looking at the list, does that seem reasonable to you?

Discuss.

• What could this list mean to us? If you were to post this list on a wall in your home, what would that suggest to you (and to others)?

That these are desirable traits, that these should be our goals, that we can aspire to develop these qualities.

• How can we attain these characteristics?

Recognize that they are gifts of the Holy Spirit and appreciate how valuable they are, pray for them, develop them through use, act them out (assume the role) until they become a part of our nature, practice—take advantage of the opportunities available and make more opportunities!

• The objective of this lesson is to encourage you to develop the fruit of the Spirit through our "root system." Who is our source of strength? Who is the gardener who cultivates our growth? The answer to these questions is found in John 15:1-8.

Ask for a volunteer to read this Scripture, or invite someone you know to be a good reader. Discuss the content.

Something to Grow By
Galatians 5:22

Something to Grow By
Galatians 5:22

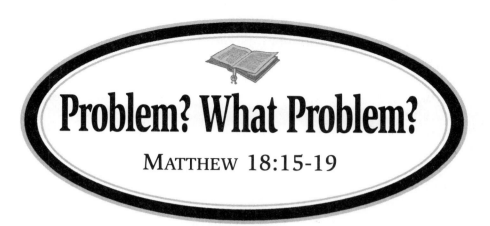

Problem? What Problem?

MATTHEW 18:15-19

To the students
- Today we're going to look at the subject of conflict resolution. Any of you ever have conflicts? Any little disagreements that you have trouble resolving? Perhaps I should ask if there is anyone in the room who doesn't have conflicts! Since we all have them, our topic today should be of interest to all of us. We're going to try to figure out if all of our conflicts are real, and if so, how to resolve them. Let's begin with a little brain exercise.

- The figures on your worksheet represent various ways that people handle conflicts—or any other kind of problem. How many can you name? Try to come up with more than one answer for each picture. For example, if you think that ostich #2 is hiding, try to think of some ways that we hide from our problems. We'll take a few minutes to do this.

- Before we continue, take a minute to jot down some current conflicts in your life. One word will suffice to remind you of the problem, without revealing anything to the person sitting next to you! Jot down a few of the things that are bothering you, and later we'll see if you have any new ideas for how to handle these problems.

Give students a few minutes to write.

- Let's go back to the worksheet and see what you have listed by each symbol.

Get input from class. Supplement discussion with material below as needed. List on a board.

Ostrich 1
Do nothing, fail to recognize the problem, ignore it, deny it, reject any suggestion of a problem.

Ostrich 2
Hide, pretend, suppress evidence, rationalize, look the other way.

Ostrich 3
Run (alternate or substitute activity), avoid (keep too busy to address, or sleep), move, change jobs, change churches.

Ostrich 4
Worry, complain, lose sleep, get an ulcer.

Ostrich 5
Face the problem, confront it, recognize own errors, faults, responsibility, consider all the facts.

• Now let's look at some biblical models for conflict resolution.

Consider ostrich 1: Do we see any biblical models for doing nothing? for ignoring a problem?
• What happened when Abram ignored the rivalry between Sarah and Hagar and between Ishmael and Isaac?
• And speaking of problems, how did Abram get in this mess in the first place?

Yes, but this approach is not recommended!
Conflicts generally tend to grow when not dealt with.

By not trusting God and waiting on his timing.

• What is the flip side of ignoring a problem?

Creating a problem where one does not exist; "making mountains out of molehills." We need to allow time to get and evaluate facts before jumping to conclusions. (There are better forms of exercise!)

• Ostrich 2: Do we see any biblical models for hiding from a problem? making excuses?

No, the Bible is quiteclear about the need to confess our sin Galatians 3:22; 1 John 1:8, 9.

• Did Adam offer an excuse when God asked him what he had done? Did his excuse work?

Yes.
No. **(Discuss.)**

• Did David make excuses for his adultery with Bathsheba?

No, he confessed and begged God's forgiveness.

• What happened with the Israelites each time they confessed their sin and turned back to God?

God forgave them and redeemed them.

• From these examples, what do we learn about the best way to deal with sin in our lives?

Humble ourselves, confess our sin, ask for God's forgiveness.

• Ostrich 3: Are there any biblical examples of running from a problem?
Did Jonah solve his problem by running from it?

Jonah.
No.

• Let's change the direction of this question just a little; does the Bible ever tell us to run from trouble before it becomes a problem?

Yes. 1 Corinthians 6:18; 10:14; 1 Timothy 6:11; 2 Timothy 2:22; James 4:7

• What does ostrich 4 represent?
• What does the Bible have to say about worry?
• Have you ever thought you had a problem only to discover later that you did not? What sorts of events or situations can make us think that there is going to be a problem? Does the Bible have anything to say about worrying about the future?

Worry.
See Matthew 6:25-34; Luke 12:22-29; 21:14
Rumors, incorrect conclusions from sparse facts, circumstantial evidence, our imagination, expectations.

• Finally we come to figure 5; facing our problem. First, we need to determine whether the conflict was caused by our own actions (or lack of action) or by someone else. Before we blame someone else, let's read Romans 8:6-8, 12:14-19; Matthew 5:21-25; 7:1-5; and Ephesians 4:25-27.

• If a person were truly able to put all these verses into practice, it's pretty hard to imagine he would ever have any personal conflict in his life! We need to be aware of the consequences of what we say and do, and be sensitive to the possibility that we may be causing the problem!

• But suppose there is a situation where you are absolutely blameless—what can you then do to resolve the situation? Matthew 18:15-19 gives us very clear instruction on how we are to handle a problem caused by a brother or sister in Christ. Let's examine this passage verse by verse.

• Verse 15 assumes you have investigated the problem and have concluded that you carry no blame. However, pointing out fault to someone else requires a very delicate approach.

• What does Ephesians 4:15 have to say about how we are to approach one another?

Ephesians 4:15 assumes that any teaching will be delivered "in love."

• So, the first step would be to kindly confront the one at fault. The King James translation of this verse suggests that the purpose for such a confrontation is to reestablish unity in the church. What negative motives might prompt us to confront someone?

To establish our superiority, to seek revenge, to prove that we were right, to make the other person feel bad

• If, after checking your motives, and after approaching your brother in love, you are unable to "win your brother over," verse 16 states that you should take "one or two others" along . . . for what purpose?

". . .so that every matter may be established by the testimony of one or two witnesses."

• This is an extremely important point. What is established by the fact that witnesses exist?

The sin was not in your imagination. The sin worthy of this approach is something more than personal offense.

• According to verse 17, what are the third and fourth steps?

Bring the matter before the church, then treat him as you would a pagan or a tax collector.

• What does this mean? If we understand "pagan" to be an unrepentant sinner, or someone who has chosen to ignore God, then we can find further clarification of this verse in 1 Corinthians 5, especially in verses 9-11. What is Paul saying here? Again it is clear that the types of sin (listed in 1 Corinthians 5) that call for this kind of discipline are not matters of personal insult or imagination.

That flagrant sin is worse in someone who knows it is sin but chooses to sin anyway. We cannot disassociate ourselves from the whole world, Paul says, but "do not even eat" (let alone worship!) with someone who calls himself a brother, but lives in sin.

• Continuing in Matthew 18, verses 18 and 19, we find yet another approach to problems. What is it?

PRAYER!

YOUR HANDOUTS ARE ON THE BACK OF THIS PAGE.
WHEN YOU PHOTOCOPY THEM, DO NOT CUT THIS PAGE APART.

Problem? What Problem?

Matthew 18:15-19

Problem? What Problem?

Matthew 18:15-19

What Do You See?

ROMANS 15:1-14

TO THE STUDENTS
• Before I tell you the objective of our study, I'd like you to look at the illustration on your worksheet and jot down whatever comes to mind. What do you see when you look at this piece of art? There are no right or wrong answers, just jot down whatever comes to mind. _____ **Give students a few minutes to write.**
• Our objective today is to examine Romans 15 and discover what we may be "seeing" in others compared to what we might better "see." We're going to take a look at positive ways to evaluate one another.

Now, what are some of the things you saw?

How many of you first noticed the spot or the "blemish." Why do you suppose we notice the blemish first? Do our thoughts usually focus where our eyes focus?

Record answers on a board.
(Blob, blemish, spot in the blob, a lot of white paper)

It seems to be where our eyes naturally focus. It may be the worst part of the blob.

• Was there more to see than the spot? Was there more to see than the blob? Some of you may have been through this exercise, or anticipated a "trick question." What else is there on this page?
• Suppose I told you that the white space represents all that is good about a person. It would be safe to say that there is generally more good about each of us than bad. Why don't we see the good that dominates someone's life?
• Just as we saw the spot in our exercise, is it also natural for us to see the "spots" (warts) in others? All too frequently the answer is "yes." Let's see what Romans 15:1-13 has to say about this.

Discuss the white space.
More of it yet we focus on the spot; "White space is boring."

Discuss.
Consider the role that the media may play in ourbeing so interested in gossip.

Read each verse and discuss. Use the following outline for help.

• Verse 1 "We who are strong ought to bear with the failings of the weak. . . ."
This verse is directed toward Christians who are expected to be strong. How strong are we? How can we grow stronger?
• Verses 1, 2 " . . . not to please ourselves. Each of us should please his neighbor for his good, to build him up."
To do this requires maturity and a positive attitude. Just as a parent should not expect a child to behave in an adult manner, mature Christians should not expect newborn Christians (or non-Christians) to always know the right thing to do. When we treat

others with kindness, patience and dignity, they are encouraged to do better. If, on the other hand, our priority is to make ourselves look good (to please ourselves) could this be because we see the "spots" in others while we believe ourselves to be spotless? **Discuss.**

• Verse 3 "Even Christ did not please himself. . . ." As always, Christ is our example. To see the example He set for us, let's read Philippians 2:6-8. **Read.**
In order to win others, teach others, lead others, we need to be able to set ourselves aside.

• Verses 4 and 5 were written to encourage Christians and give a spirit of unity so that . . .

• Verse 6 ". . . with one heart and mouth you may glorify the God and Father of our Lord Jesus Christ. "
Can God be glorified by a church at war with itself? If the body of Christ is divided—arguing, finding fault with one another—will God be glorified? Could this be a major reason why we are told not to judge one another? **Discuss.**

• Verse 7 "Accept one another, then, just as Christ accepted you, . . ."
How did Christ accept us? Did He require us to get straightened out before He loved us? Did He require us to clean up our act before He died for us?
We are to accept others—warts and all!—"in order to bring praise to God."
How can we do this?
Discuss, incorporating the following:

Speak well of others (don't discuss the spots). Don't be critical (see James 4:11 and Luke 6:41, 42). Look for good things to say about everyone. Look for ways to be helpful. Give full consideration to the ideas of others. (Is our way the only way?) Try to really understand other points of view. When in doubt, give others the benefit. Forgive. Look beyond the obvious—especially the warts!

• Verses 8-12 Paul returns to the theme of Christ's servanthood, specifically to the Jews, which confirmed "the promises made to the patriarchs so that the Gentiles may glorify God for his mercy."
Understanding that salvation in Christ was offered first to the Jews, and that "Gentiles" meant anyone who was not a Jew, how can we apply this verse today? How does unity in the church—unity among Christians—give Gentiles (unbelievers) reason to glorify God? For help on this, turn to 1 Peter 2:12.
Read and discuss.

• The flip side of this, of course, is that dissension among Christians causes unbelievers to laugh, not only at Christians, but at God. If we cannot even love each other, how can we be trusted to love "outsiders"?

• What are some of the reasons we have so much trouble loving each other?
Discuss pride and jealousy.

CONCLUSIONS
1. Accepting one another glorifies God.
2. Acceptance entails positive attitudes and actions.
3. Most of us have to work at getting away from our natural focus on faults.

What Do You See?
Romans 15:1-14

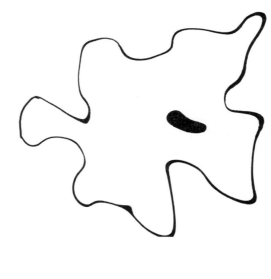

What Do You See?
Romans 15:1-14

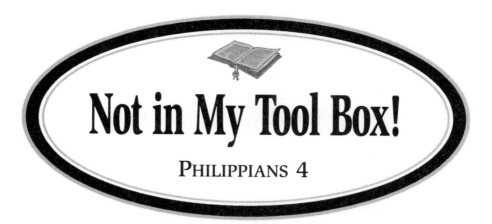

Not in My Tool Box!

PHILIPPIANS 4

TO THE STUDENTS

• Today you have an opportunity to let your imaginations go wild! I want you to list at least five things that come to mind when you look at this illustration.

• The objective of our class time today is to evaluate the way we think about things—especially our tendency to judge new or different ideas. First, let's make a list of your comments about the illustration.

FOR THE TEACHER

Distribute worksheet. Give students time to put down some ideas. List comments on a board. Supplement student comments with list below if necessary. Disregard the symbols for now.

- − *Crazy!*
- o *Different*
- + *Has multiple purposes*
- + *May be useful—do two jobs at once*
- − *Not practical*
- o *Limited edition*
- − *Looks funny*
- + *Foundation for other tools*
- o *Appears to be several tools in one*
- − *Unusable (How about a boat anchor?)*
- − *You crazy? Not in my tool box!*

• Now let's turn to Philippians 4 and read verses 2-9. Look at verses 2-6. In the New International Bible, this section of Scripture is titled "Exhortations." Let's go through these verses and list all the exhortations.

Read. Pronunciation: You-O-di-us, SIN-tih-key
List on the board:

- *agree with each other*
- *help these women*
- *rejoice in the Lord*
- *let your gentleness be evident to all*
- *do not be anxious*
- *with thanksgiving, present your request to God.*

• What is the mood or feeling of all these directions? Do these instructions seem worthwhile, beneficial?

They are all very positive. Good advice. Good attitudes to strive for.

• Now let's read verse eight and list all the key words on the board.

• What do these words mean? Give me some synonyms for each word.

- *true - honest, right, best, straight*
- *noble - lofty, grand, high ideals*
- *right - correct, source of truth, virtuous*
- *pure - unblemished, blameless*
- *lovely - attractive, pretty, pleasant*
- *admirable - excellent, splendid, deserving praise*
- *excellent - of highest quality*
- *praiseworthy - worth talking about, worth sharing*

• Are these things negative or positive?

Positive!

• Looking at our list, do we have more negatives or more positives? Granted, this was not the best illustration for generating positive responses, but it was designed to help us think a little.

Negatives.

• How do we generally respond to new ideas? When your spouse, or roommate, or coworker says, "I have an idea!" what is your gut reaction? Why is it that we seem to be programmed to expect the worst? When someone presents a new idea in a committee meeting, what are the initial reactions of the people there?

Oh no!

"That will never work," "That's the stupidest thing I ever heard!"

• Suppose I were to tell you that this tool is not what it seems to be. Perhaps it is several different tools all jumbled up in a pile. Or, on closer examination, perhaps we would find that each part was removable. Perhaps this is actually a replica of a sculpture by a famous artist that sold for $25,000 and now sits on the lawn of a millionaire! Would any of these explanations change your perception of the tool?

- *Things are not always as they seem*
- *We may need to look more carefully for positives*
- *Re-evaluations may be helpful*
- *Our instruction from the Word is to be positive*
- *We may need practice to break old habits*
- *We need to think before we speak*
- *Avoid negatives and actively pursue the positives*
- *Maybe this tool should be in our toolbox—as a reminder that things are not always what they seem!*

• Let's share some conclusions we can draw from this discussion. Keeping Philippians 4:2-9 in mind, what adjustments could we make to our typical responses (about the tool and about things in general)?

• A story is told of a minister who had a reputation for saying only good things about people in his small town. When the village reprobate died this minister was asked to conduct the funeral service. The whole town showed up to see if the minister could live up to his reputation and find something good to say about the deceased. They were surprised but not disappointed when he related, "The man had a very good set of teeth."
• What is the point of this story? What thoughts can we take home with us today about how we think about others?

Discuss.

Not in My Tool Box!

Philippians 4

Not in My Tool Box!

Philippians 4

Hide or Seek?

EPHESIANS 5:8-17

TO THE STUDENTS

• The big sunburst on your worksheet represents God's will. Draw a path to this sunburst that represents your journey toward finding God's will. For example, has your search been a straight path from ignorance to knowledge? Have you wandered a bit, been distracted? Have you hit roadblocks? Have you turned away from the search?

Allow students time to think and draw.

• Next we have two timelines representing the distance between you and God's will. Place a mark on the first line that shows how close you are to *knowing* God's will. Place a mark on the second line that shows how close you are to *doing* God's will.

• Are the two marks in different places? Why?

Discuss.

• When we read the accounts in the Old Testament it is sometimes tempting to wonder why "those people" had so much trouble obeying God. After all, the Israelites experienced the power of God when they lived through the ten plagues and when they left Egypt. They *saw* God's mighty presence in the pillar of cloud and of fire. They *ate* the food that God sent from Heaven and *drank* the water that He brought from a rock! How could they doubt Him? Even Gideon, who had direct conversation with an angel of God, needed more proof that he was hearing the will of God before he believed! We might tend to think, "Wow! If God ever spoke to me, I'd have no trouble obeying Him!" Today we will consider whether or not that is true.

• Our objectives today will be first, to discover whether or not God really wants us to know His will, and second, to transform our knowing into doing. Let's start by reading Ephesians 5:8-17.

Read.

• Do you believe God wants us to walk in His will? Is God's will hidden from us? Look again at verses 10 and 17. Do you think God would instruct us (through Paul) to "understand what the Lord's will is" if this were an impossible task?

Discuss.

• Look at the verses surrounding 8-17—the section we read. What do you find in verses 1-7 and 18 through the end of the chapter—in fact, through the end of Ephesians? Is this clearly the will of God?

Complete and detailed lists of things we are to do and are not to do. Yes!

• Let's look at 1 Thessalonians 5:16, 17.

Read.

• All the verses surrounding this statement also clearly state the will of God. In fact, this is pretty much what the Bible is about! Is knowing God's will really a problem?

• Do you believe it is necessary to seek God's will in all decisions? What about these situations:
1. What you will have for lunch
2. Where you will eat lunch
3. Whom you will invite to eat lunch with you
4. Which job you will accept
5. Where you live
6. What car you drive
7. Whom you marry

• Do you notice any kind of a progression here? Does it seem that the more important the decision, the more we need to seek God's will? Does God care about the kind of car we drive? Before you answer, ask yourself these questions:
1. "Am I looking for transportation from place to place, or a status symbol?"
2. "Could I buy a less expensive car and give the money saved to help others?"
3. "Is my car just a mode of transportation or an extension of myself?"
4. "Am I secretly pleased when I own a more expensive car than my neighbor?"

• Consider this: Does God's will have more to do with our attitudes than our actions? Isn't it true that if our attitudes are right, right actions will follow? **(Discuss.)** While we use our own will in making choices, God's will clearly should impact all of our decisions.

• When we have trouble doing God's will we need to ask ourselves if our problem is knowing what God's will is, not knowing how to accomplish it, or not being willing to obey God's will. **(Discuss.)**

• Let's read some of the reassurances we have that God wants to guide us. These references are listed on your worksheet. Psalm 32:8; 73:24; Proverbs 3:5, 6; Romans 12:2; Colossians 1:9; James 1:5, 6.

• Continuing on your worksheet, let's look up these Scriptures and list some of the principles that help us do God's will.

SCRIPTURE	PRINCIPLE
Romans 12:1, 2	Be available always to carry out God's will (be a living sacrifice).
1 John 5:14	Get serious about prayer. Do you believe God's Word? Are you serious about your request? Then pray with confidence and boldness.
Matthew 5:3-12; 6:33	Get your priorities straight; value what God values.
Galatians 5:16-26	Be led by the Spirit.
1 Timothy 3	Be obedient to God's Word. This passage in particular calls for maturity.
Psalm 1:1, 2	Seek counsel, not only from God, but from other godly sources.
Romans 8:28	Know that if you are honestly trying to live for God, He will work in every seemingly bad situation to bring about good. (Can you think of some experiences that make more sense when looking back on them?)
2 Peter 3:8, 9	Be patient. God's concept of time is radically different from ours. (Discuss how the world seeks instant gratification in everything.)
Luke 18:1	Be persistent in prayer, in seeking God's will. Pray until God clearly answers "no." Then, don't try to go through doors that are closed (you would clearly be outside of God's will).
2 Timothy 2:15	Do your best. Study God's Word—then relax and let the Holy Spirit work.

• Now, let's talk about the paths we drew to illustrate our search for God's will. I don't want to get too personal, so don't answer if you don't want to!

• Do our paths indicate that we are seriously, honestly seeking God's will? Is it possible that some of us are afraid to seek God's will, or would just rather not know what He wants us to do?

• Did any of you draw multiple paths to God's will? This is a good answer, because as we have seen from our study, there are multiple ways to discover God's will. When we find an intersection, or agreement, of various biblical principles, and our decision is confirmed by the counsel of godly people, we can rest assured that we have come to a place that God wants us to be. When honestly seeking God's will, we should come to a place where we see things "come together."

ADDITIONAL POINTS TO PONDER

• Do we make up our mind to do or not do something regardless of what message we get from God?

• If you seek God's will are you willing to obey when you find it?

• Just as we learn to trust others, we can learn to trust God. Review your experience with God and His providence—is He trustworthy?

• When seeking God's will, double check—think twice, act once.

EXPERIENCE SHARING

What experiences are you willing to share in discerning God's will in your life? What decisions are you facing?

Hide or Seek?

| You | Knowing | God's Will |

| You | Doing | God's Will |

Reassurances: Psalm 32:8; 73:24; Proverbs 3:5, 6; Romans 12:2; Colossians 1:9; James 1:5, 6

Scripture	Principle
Romans 12:1, 2	
1 John 5:14	
Matthew 5:3-12	
Galatians 5:16-26	
1 Timothy 3	
Psalm 1:1, 2	
Romans 8:28	
2 Peter 3:8, 9	
Luke 18:1	

Hide or Seek?

| You | Knowing | God's Will |

| You | Doing | God's Will |

Reassurances: Psalm 32:8; 73:24; Proverbs 3:5, 6; Romans 12:2; Colossians 1:9; James 1:5, 6

Scripture	Principle
Romans 12:1, 2	
1 John 5:14	
Matthew 5:3-12	
Galatians 5:16-26	
1 Timothy 3	
Psalm 1:1, 2	
Romans 8:28	
2 Peter 3:8, 9	
Luke 18:1	

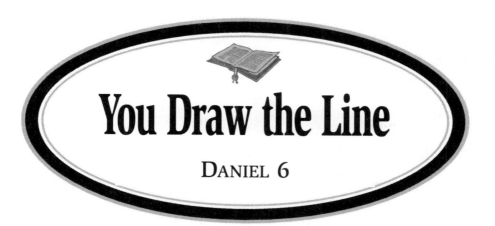

You Draw the Line

DANIEL 6

To the students

• Let's suppose that the blank portion of your worksheet represents your life—this blank page is who you are! Somewhere in this square I want you to draw a line, or a symbol that represents your convictions, or your standards. In other words, where do you "draw the line"? Are you consistent in where you draw the line? There is no "correct" place or way to draw the line. This is just an exercise to generate thought and discussion.

For the teacher

Allow time to draw.

• Today we want to examine the fact that in our acceptance or rejection of ideas we all "draw lines," either consciously or subconsciously. We'll look at what elements are used, or should be used in determining where we "draw the line." We'll read Daniel 6 for our biblical resource.

• First, let's look at the lines we drew. Perhaps a trained psychologist could give us some reasons of why we drew the lines where we did. But trained or not, let's just come up with some possibilities.

List examples and/or draw lines on board, discuss possible meanings.

1. Horizontal line drawn high: High standards, no compromise
2. Horizontal line drawn low: Low standards, low expectations, procrastinator?
3. Horizontal line in the middle: Middle of the road, not sure (no instructions)
4. Jagged line: Innovative, experimental, cover more area
5. Square box: Compartmentalized thinking, ("Sunday is for church!"); controlled
6. Other

• Does anyone have any idea why you drew the line the way or place that you did? We may not be able to describe why we drew the line where we did, but there is probably some underlying reason. Perhaps our general behavior fits the same pattern.

Discuss.

• Now let's take a look at where Daniel drew the line. Turn to Daniel 6.
• Daniel was taken from Jerusalem to Babylon as a captive in the earliest days of the great Babylonian empire. He was brilliant, diligent in his duties, and under the special care of God. He was absolutely unswerving in his religious convictions and practice. He served throughout the reigns of King Nebuchadnezzar and his son, King Belshazzar, throughout the reign of Darius the Mede

who took over the kingdom, and into the reign of King Cyrus. Throughout these years his reputation grew as one who could be trusted, and as one who had been given interpretive powers by his God. King Darius called on Daniel to interpret the message that appeared on his wall at his banquet. Daniel read the prediction of death to King Darius and the division of his kingdom, and the prediction was fulfilled that night. This event gave birth to the expression, "the handwriting is on the wall," which we use to mean that the destruction of someone or something is near at hand.

• In the early part of chapter 6 we see that Daniel had become a high official to King Darius and had shown such ability that the king planned to set him over the whole kingdom (v. 3). Apparently, jealousy among the other leaders led them to plot the death of Daniel. By appealing to the king's vanity, they got him to sign a decree that no one was to pray to anyone except the king for 30 days. The punishment for disobeying this decree was that the offender would be thrown into the lions' den.

• In verse 10 we see that Daniel continued his practice of daily prayer, getting down on his knees before an open window where all could see him. He was an easy target for his enemies, who dragged him before the king and demanded that he be thrown into the lions' den. When the king realized he had been tricked, verse 14 says he was "greatly distressed" and "determined to rescue Daniel." But the jealous officials used the king's own law against him and Darius was forced to throw Daniel to the lions. But of course, we all know what happened! In verse 19 we find that God did indeed protect Daniel; the king had him released and replaced by his accusers. The king then issued another decree that people must fear and reverence the God of Daniel (v. 26). And Daniel prospered again (v. 28).

• Where did Daniel draw the line?

Where man's law conflicted with his commitment.

• Verse 10 reveals Daniel's standard, his position on the matter. Please read Daniel 6:10.

He prayed, "just as he had done before"—the decree made no difference to him.

• There's another clue in verse 16. Please read.

Everyone in the land, including the king, knew of Daniel's commitment to his God.

• Did it make any difference to Daniel that he knew he would be caught?

Perhaps. We should not gloss over this. Daniel was just a man. The prospect of being eaten alive was no doubt terrifying. But he was not willing to compromise his devotion to God.

• What are some of the elements that determined where Daniel drew the line?

• *His character*
• *His love of, devotion to God*
• *His background and training*
• *His surroundings*

• What did his surrounding have to do with his commitment to God? What do we know about the faith of persecuted Christians?

Daniel and the other captives were in a heathen land. If they didn't stand for God, no one would. When your back is up against the wall, your true character shows. Perhaps we have it too easy.

• Does this have a message for us?

Discuss.

• We might be enormously relieved that we are not being persecuted for being Christians, but perhaps we should take a closer look at this issue. The Bible takes the point of view that if you are a Christian, you will be persecuted. See the verses listed on your worksheet. Perhaps the question we need to ask is, "Why am I not suffering for Christ?"

Discuss:
Matthew 10:22; Luke 6:22, 23; 1 Peter 3:14; 4:16; 5:8-10; Romans 5:3,4; 8:18; 2 Timothy 1:8; 3:12; and James 5:10, 11.

• One of the popular buzzwords today is "tolerance." "We need to be more tolerant of lifestyle choices," some say. But God sets forth very definite standards of right and wrong and we frequently bump into areas where we need to draw lines. When we do, do we draw those lines in different places? Are we more tolerant of some sins than of others?

• Do we have a tendency to rate some of these sins as less sinful than others? Why is that? Does God "rate" sin? See James 2:10, 11; 1 John 3: 4.

• What determines where we draw the line?

• There are many things that shape our lives and help us set our standards—and they are not all good. We need to examine the influences on our minds and see if they help us conform to God's will or the world's will (see Romans 12:1, 2).

1. Honesty and integrity: Self-protecting "white lies," reporting all our income to the government, reporting a mistake in our favor to the bank or supermarket clerk
2. Work ethics: Putting in a full day's work, using company equipment for personal business, creating dissension among co-workers
3. Homosexuality
4. TV programs/books/magazines: Do we condemn others for using pornography while we fill our minds with amoral trash?
5. Abortion
6. Domestic violence: Verbal, emotional, physical
7. Obeying traffic laws

1. Upbringing
2. Education
3. Family values
4. Strength of will, character
5. Church experience/biblical knowledge
6. Culture
7. Our own comfort level (whether or not the sin costs us or interferes with our lives)

• In conclusion I would simply remind you that the God who took away King Nebuchadnezzar's mind because he was full of pride and the God who saved Daniel from being ripped to pieces by hungry lions is the same God we serve today. Has His power grown weaker? Is He any less angered by sin (even the sin of pride)?   **Discuss.**

• Daniel followed a life pattern pleasing to God in spite of the consequences. When he openly worshiped God in heathen surroundings, God blessed him. When he placed his life squarely in God's hands, God protected him. Is it possible that if we exhibited the faith and courage of Daniel we might see God working in our lives in a more miraculous fashion?   **Discuss.**

• There are two questions at the bottom of the worksheet for us to answer privately and think about during our quiet times this week. Let's ask God to strengthen our resolve and help us grow in these areas.

YOUR HANDOUTS ARE ON THE BACK OF THIS PAGE. WHEN YOU PHOTOCOPY THEM, DO NOT CUT THIS PAGE.

You Draw the Line

Daniel 6

Do these verses apply to me? If not, why not?
Matthew 10:22; Luke 6:22, 23; 1 Peter 3:14; 4:16; 5:8-10; Romans 5:3,4; 8:18; 2 Timothy 1:8; 3:12; James 5:10, 11

In what areas of my life have I become too tolerant?

What are some things I can do this week to set my standards closer to God's?

You Draw the Line

Daniel 6

Do these verses apply to me? If not, why not?
Matthew 10:22; Luke 6:22, 23; 1 Peter 3:14; 4:16; 5:8-10; Romans 5:3,4; 8:18; 2 Timothy 1:8; 3:12; James 5:10, 11

In what areas of my life have I become too tolerant?

What are some things I can do this week to set my standards closer to God's?

What Seed Is This?

JUDGES 9

To the students

• On our worksheets today we have a picture of a seed. What kind of seed do you think this could be?

For the teacher

Allow time for discussion.

• If you were to find a seed and plant it, would it matter what kind it is?

Yes. We like to know what to expect. A tree planted too close to the house could destroy the foundation. Or, the plant could be marijuana!

• What kinds of seeds do we plant? I'm thinking now of both literal and figurative seeds. Think of some expressions using the word, "seed."

• *Garden/farm varieties*
• *Wild oats*
• *Seed money for new enterprises*
• *Seeds of doubt or discontent*
• *Seeds that generate thoughts or actions in others*
• *Seeds of disobedience*

• Do we always reap what we sow? Do we always reap the full punishment (or reward) for what we've done?

No, it seems that grace comes into play even in this world. We may say or do something that could hurt someone but by the grace of God they never find out about it—or they may find out but forgive us. But even in that case, trust is usually damaged—cutting words will always leave a scar.

• Suppose you have sown some corrupt seed but recognized your error and are sorry for your actions—what then?

• *You may still have to pay for any damages caused*
• *There may be legal ramifications*
• *Your reputation will be damaged*
• *The pain that you caused will not go away just because you are sorry*

• What are some corrupt seeds we see planted when the person thinks he will "get away with it"?

• *"Creative" income tax returns*
• *Cheating on a spouse*
• *Petty theft*
• *Overcharging for goods or services*
• *White lies*

• Let's turn to Galatians 6:7, 8 and see what God has to say about sowing seeds.

Read and discuss.

• The difference between how the world holds us accountable and how God holds us accountable is of course that He sees everything, He is a just God, and He has promised that there will be a day of judgment (Matthew 12:36). So, our objective today is to help each other identify the seeds we sow and to see that we will reap according. We will also identify ways we think we can disobey God and not suffer the consequences. We are going to use Abimelech as our biblical example. Please turn to Judges 9.

ABIMELECH'S STORY

• Apparently Abimelech thought he could plant radish seeds and harvest tomatoes. (They do look similar—both are round and red.) He thought he could disobey God and still be blessed. Abimelech was the son of Gideon by a slave woman. Although Gideon lived like a king, he refused to establish a dynasty. Abimelech decided that was an error and set out to make himself king. He lived in Shechem where both Israelites and Canaanites lived. While Abimelech's seventy half brothers had been born to Israelite women, his mother was a Shechemite. His father, Gideon, also know as Jerub-Baal, was an Israelite. Therefore, it probably seemed politically expedient that Abimelech could represent both sides of the family and not be as partial as his seventy half brothers.

• After getting the support and approval of his mother's family, Abimelech hired reckless adventurers (v. 4) who proceeded to his father's home in Oprah to assist Abimelech in murdering his seventy brothers. Only the youngest (Jotham) escaped. In verses 7 to 20 we read the parable of the "thornbush." (Here is an example that not all parables are found in the New Testament.)

• By verse 23 we find that God begins to even the score. Abimelech's power begins to wane. In his last rampage of taking over and burning cities and people, a woman dropped a millstone on his head. A woman! In that culture, to be killed by a woman was considered a very low blow. To save face, he asked his armorbearer to run him through so people could not say that a woman had killed him.

• What seeds were sown by Abimelech? How many of the ten commandments did he break? (They are listed on your worksheet.)

Discuss the questions and encourage answers. Remember, the answers below are only for suggestions if the class gets stuck.

1. *You shall have no other gods before me. Abimelech was serving several gods: himself, power, ambition, might.*
2. *You shall not make for yourself an idol. We see in Judges 9:4 that Abimelech accepted money from Baal worshipers. Would this have pleased God?*
5. *Honor your father and your mother, so that you may live long. His father, Gideon, was an honorable man. Did Abimelech follow in his steps? honor his memory?*
6. *You shall not murder. Abimelech started his career by murdering his seventy brothers. He continued by destroying everyone in every city he wanted.*
10. *You shall not covet. Discuss ambition compared to obsession and being aggressive versus being obnoxious.*

• Did Abimelech reap what he had sown?

Yes. He had trouble defending and retaining his kingdom. Citizens of Shechem cursed him (v. 27). He lost his kingdom (vs. 50-57). He died a shameful death (also see 2 Samuel 11:21).

• Admittedly, our life situations are considerably different from Abimelech's. None of us is in the political position to murder our family in order to ascend to power, or sack the neighboring cities to expand our kingdoms! But the underlying temptations are the same. We can be tempted by the allure of power, we have probably all "thrown our weight around" at some point or another. We would probably go to great lengths to protect our reputation, and many of us have experienced sibling rivalry.

• The bottom line is that we need to carefully evaluate the seeds that we sow.

What are some ways to make sure we sow better seeds?

1. Identify what we are sowing. Study God's Word so that we can do this.
2. Think about our words and actions and their consequences before they occur.
3. Reflect on past words and actions and work out corrections. Rectify past "misplants" as much as possible.
4. Take less for granted. Be sure people know what we mean by our words and actions.
5. Check our attitudes. Are we sorry when we've done wrong or sorry that we got caught?
6. Seek forgiveness of God and man.

• We've been talking about sowing the right kind of seeds, but the verse I'd like to conclude with has more to do with continuing productivity. This verse is on your worksheets; let's read it together:

"Sow your seed in the morning, and at evening let not your hands be idle, for you do not know which will succeed, whether this or that, or whether both will do equally well."

Ecclesiastes 11:6

YOUR HANDOUTS ARE ON THE BACK OF THIS PAGE.
WHEN YOU PHOTOCOPY THEM, DO NOT CUT THIS PAGE APART.

33

What Seed Is This?

Judges 6

1. You shall have no other gods before me.
2. You shall not make for yourself an idol.
3. You shall not misuse the name of the Lord your God.
4. Remember the Sabbath day by keeping it holy.
5. Honor your father and your mother,
   so that you may live long.
6. You shall not murder.
7. You shall not commit adultery.
8. You shall not steal.
9. You shall not give false testimony.
10. You shall not covet.

"Sow your seed in the morning, and at evening let not your hands be idle, for you do not know which will succeed, whether this or that, or whether both will do equally well."
Ecclesiastes 11:6

What Seed Is This?

Judges 6

1. You shall have no other gods before me.
2. You shall not make for yourself an idol.
3. You shall not misuse the name of the Lord your God.
4. Remember the Sabbath day by keeping it holy.
5. Honor your father and your mother,
   so that you may live long.
6. You shall not murder.
7. You shall not commit adultery.
8. You shall not steal.
9. You shall not give false testimony.
10. You shall not covet.

"Sow your seed in the morning, and at evening let not your hands be idle, for you do not know which will succeed, whether this or that, or whether both will do equally well."
Ecclesiastes 11:6

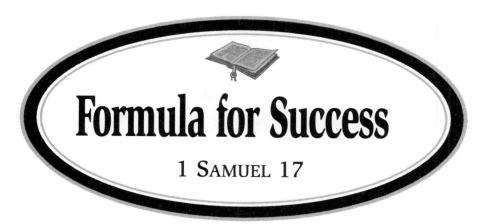

Formula for Success

1 SAMUEL 17

TO THE STUDENTS
• This is the age of computers and high tech everything. This graphic is directed toward all the math wizards or computer gurus who may be into formulation. The cryptic message on your worksheet is a formula for solving problems. Take just a few minutes to see if you can decipher the formula.

FOR THE TEACHER
Hand out student worksheets and give the students only a few minutes to work on the code.

• 1 Samuel 17 contains the well-known account of the encounter between the youth, David, and the giant, Goliath. Our objective is to use this popular story to examine our approach to problem solving.

• First, let's talk about success. What is success? What words, or feelings describe success for you?

Wait for class responses and list on the board. The following are some suggestions. After listing, discuss what they are.
1. Happiness—elusive concept, optimism
2. Freedom from anxiety/worry
3. Accomplishment/achievement—even simple tasks
4. Completing a task—overcoming obstacles
5. Knowing God's will
6. Favorable outcome—what's good, right, best
7. Other

• How do we measure success?

1. Financial gain
2. Attaining a reward—Heaven, for the Christian
3. Mastering our problems
4. Satisfaction—warm fuzzy feeling
5. Other

• Unfortunately, our society is geared toward measuring success by financial gain. However, even the world discovers that money is not the source of real happiness. Perhaps you have seen some of those interviews with people who have received hundreds of thousands of dollars from lotteries, or contests, or from inheritances. Many of them agree that beyond the initial stage of excitement, they did not feel more happy or successful. In some cases the money ruined their lives. Some reported that friends and even family members had deserted them because of struggles over the money. This is not to say that financial success is to be considered a negative. I want to point out only that getting wads of money will not necessarily solve our problems.
• Now, let's decode this formula that may help us with all sorts of challenges.

Encourage answers from the students. Fill in the missing answers. Do not spend a lot of time on this step. You will come back to this after an overview of the Scripture.

P =	O =	A =	PS =	Aa =	S =
problem	*obstacles*	*advantages*	*possible solutions*	*action*	*solution*

You might let class members supply the elements of the story, asking questions to elicit key points.

SYNOPSIS OF 1 SAMUEL 17:1-58

• Israel was at war with the Philistines, as they had been for more than 60 years (Judges 13:1; 1 Samuel 7:2). The Israelites were camped on one side of the Valley of Elah and the Philistines were on the other. But this time, rather than engaging both armies in combat, the Philistines thought they had a "champion" (v. 4), and they saw an opportunity to humiliate the Israelites. Goliath stood over nine feet tall and his armor weighed about 150 pounds. His spear head weighed about 20 pounds. Every day this giant would challenge one Israelite to fight him. He shouted insults across the valley, ridiculing the army by saying, in effect, "Is there not one single *man* among you?"

• The challenge was: one battle between Goliath and one Israelite—winner take all. However, King Saul and his army were dismayed and terrified (v. 11). This challenge was repeated for 40 days! During this time, David was directed by his father, Jesse, to take food to the camp and bring back a report of his three brothers. Instead of bringing back a report, David took up the challenge against Goliath with only his sling, five stones, and great faith in his heavenly Father. As we know, he was successful in triumphing over the giant (v. 50) and the Israelites became the victor.

• How can we apply David's strategy to our formula? First, he recognized the problem. This is an important step. We can't make any wise decisions about

what to do in any situation unless we fully understand the problem.

1. RECOGNIZE THE PROBLEM.
• David could see how big Goliath was (v. 23). He also heard the defiant challenge that insulted "the armies of the living God" (v. 26). David was "righteously indignant."
• Is there a difference between defending someone else, or their reputation, and in defending yourself? David was indignant that this "uncircumcised Philistine" (heathen) should defame God's people and he wanted to do something to "remove this disgrace from Israel" (v. 26). David also knew that Goliath was a skilled warrior—if David hadn't come to that conclusion himself, the king told him (v. 33)!

• David had some other problems to deal with beside these physical realities. The entire Israelite army was terrified of Goliath—wouldn't such mass hysteria have some effect on David? Furthermore, his oldest brother, Eliab, was furious at David's presence and no doubt suspected what his precocious kid brother would do. After all, David had been chosen by God to be Israel's next king and Eliab and all the other brothers had seen Samuel anoint David. Eliab's jealously was raging (v. 28).

• Do the fears and opinions of others influence our attitudes, our ability to handle a problem? **Discuss.**

2. ADD TO THE ORIGINAL PROBLEM THE OBSTACLES IN SOLVING IT.

• Goliath was huge. David was small. He couldn't change those obstacles. As for the fear of the army, instead of allowing it to undermine his courage, David apparently chose to ignore it—he never even addressed it. And he treated his brother's jealousy with light-hearted indifference (v. 29) and "turned away to someone else" (v. 30). In other words, he refused to let his brother pick a fight. David's quick response suggests that he had had plenty of practice in dealing with this kind of comment from his brother. Just think of his incredible situation: he'd been anointed king, but his father had him out watching the sheep while his big brothers went off to war! A lesser man might have turned bitter in this situation, but David knew he was being groomed, or molded by God (16:13).

• What can you and I learn from this?
Discuss

3. SUBTRACT YOUR ADVANTAGES —YOUR TALENTS AND ATTRIBUTES.

Confidence in the Lord. Every word out of David's mouth exudes confidence—in the Lord. He never claims any might or power of his own (vv. 32, 34-37, 39, 45-47).

Character. A petty man might lord his position over his brothers. But David chose not to take offense at his brother's insults. It takes a mighty man to realize that he does not need to defend his own position of power.

Proper assessment of your experience and skills. David had killed lions and bears with his bare hands (v. 34-37), yet he was quick to point out that this ability came from God. Just so, he told the king, "the Lord will deliver me from the hand of this Philistine" (v. 37). David's calm courage (v. 32) came from his *experience* with God. He had experi-

enced the power of God and he trusted God to be with him again.

• Do we exhibit this same depth of faith?
Discuss

• At the same time, when King Saul wanted David to wear his own armor, David put it on and "tried walking around." That must have been a funny sight because we know from 1 Samuel 9:2 that Saul was an "impressive young man without equal among the Israelites —a head taller than any of the others," and we can infer from 1 Samuel 16:6-12 that David was not as tall as any of his brothers. So here we have David struggling to wear Saul's armor and he rightly assesses that these garments would only hamper him. Instead, he chooses the weapons that he is accustomed to using and he knows he can use well—his staff, his sling, and five smooth stones.

• There is a good lesson in this for us. We need to have confidence in the skills that God has given us, and use them to the best of our ability instead of trying to copy someone else.

4. DIVIDE YOUR OBSTACLES AND ADVANTAGES BY YOUR POSSIBLE SOLUTIONS.

• One solution would have been to concede the battle to Goliath—give up. Who knows what might have happened if David had not shown up? Reminds me of another saying, "Not to decide is to decide not to." In other words, if we don't take action to solve a problem, it will solve itself—and perhaps in a very distasteful manner!

• Another possible solution would have been to send Israelite soldiers out, one at a time, to face Goliath. Everyone was certain what the outcome of that would be! At least King Saul was wise enough not to sacrifice his men like that. Do we ever waste our resources by "throwing good money after bad," or by continuing to do the same old thing when it has already been proven not to work? **Discuss**

• As we have already seen, David considered wearing Saul's armor. This would have been attacking the problem in the expected manner. We put a lot of stock in tried and true solutions and in what has worked for other people. Maybe in these situations we need to step back and listen more carefully for God's way.
The solution David chose was to place his faith in God and use his own best abilities.

5. TAKE ACTION
• David assessed the situation, weighed his options, made his decision and then he took action. We can't be certain from the biblical account, but it seems as if all this occurred on the day that David arrived on the scene. Possibly not, because between the time that David heard Goliath's challenge and he responded to it, some men in the army reported David's interest to the king and the king "sent for him." At any rate, not a great deal of time passed.
• We can also draw from this account that David didn't spend any time fussing and fuming over the problem. He saw what needed to be done, he had confidence in the Lord's ability to see him through, and he responded.
• David's confidence and courage up to this point certainly deserves our admiration, but look what he did next: standing within earshot of both armies, facing this nine-foot giant who is furious that a boy has answered his challenge, David publicly calls on the power of God and calmly states the outcome of the battle, "This day the Lord will hand you over to me, and I'll strike you down and cut off your head" (v. 46).

• What gave David that kind of faith? Is it possible to have that kind of faith today? Why don't we see more of it? Do we, or do we not have confidence in the Lord? Do we believe that the Lord God is able to handle our problems? What keeps us from acting on that belief?
Discuss

• The problem, plus obstacles, minus advantages, divided by possible solutions, plus action, equals solution: David finished the job. He was ready, willing, and able, and God was with him.

CONCLUSIONS
• Read with me the verses on the bottom of your worksheet, "Keep your lives free from the love of money and be content with what you have, because God has said, 'Never will I leave you; never will I forsake you.' So we say with confidence, 'The Lord is my helper; I will not be afraid. What can man do to me?'"

• Stop for a minute and think about the power behind that promise. **(Pause.)**
• Young children are blissfully free of problems. They are totally dependent on their caregivers. They do not worry about their needs because they trust their parents to supply them. We are called to be "children of God." We know God is trustworthy—more so than any earthly parent! What keeps us from trusting Him? Why do we so often feel helpless? Why do we feel overwhelmed by our problems?

• From our lesson today, what steps can we take when facing a problem?

1. Spend some time analyzing the problem.
2. Seek God's help and wisdom.
3. Consider alternatives—old solutions, new ideas, suggestions of others.
4. Trust God, have faith and confidence in Him and in the abilities He has given to you.
5. "Just do it."

Formula for Success

1 Samuel 17

$$P\left(\frac{+0 \cdot A}{PS}\right) + Aa = S$$

P
+0
-A
÷PS
+Aa
=S

"Keep your lives free from the love of money and be content with what you have, because God has said, 'Never will I leave you; never will I forsake you.' So we say with confidence, 'The Lord is my helper; I will not be afraid. What can man do to me?'"

Hebrews 13:5, 6

Formula for Success

1 Samuel 17

$$P\left(\frac{+0 \cdot A}{PS}\right) + Aa = S$$

P
+0
-A
÷PS
+Aa
=S

"Keep your lives free from the love of money and be content with what you have, because God has said, 'Never will I leave you; never will I forsake you.' So we say with confidence, 'The Lord is my helper; I will not be afraid. What can man do to me?'"

Hebrews 13:5, 6

What's Wrong With This Picture?

MATTHEW 25:21

• On your handout today is a loose translation of a familiar Bible verse from the NIV®. Before you look up the reference, take a few minutes and change the words that you know are wrong.

"Well thought out, smart and considerate person! You have done pretty well with a few things; I will consider you for a few more. Come, let's ponder your boss's happiness."

Provide a few minutes, then suggest that the students look up the Scripture and finish their editing.

"Well done, good and faithful servant! You have been faithful with a few things; I will put you in charge of many things. Come and share your master's happiness!"

• How many of the differences were you able to pick out before looking up the Scripture? Were you surprised by some you missed? Let's go over the changes and discuss the differences between the two. Look especially for the changes from passive thought to action. Our objective is to challenge ourselves to put our spoken or professed faith into action.

"well thought out" versus "well done"	*Is thinking or planning the same as doing? On what will we be judged?*
"smart" versus "good"	*Is a smart person as beneficial to others as a good person? When we judge a person "good," are we generally evaluating their thoughts or their actions?*
"semi-reliable" versus "faithful"	*Which would you rather have for a car—or a spouse? How much can the Lord count on us?*
"person" versus "servant"	*This one is hard. Read 1 Corinthians 6:19, 20. If we thought of ourselves as servants, what to do with "our" time, "our" talents, "our" money would not be much of a problem. If we are servants then we need to be serving.*
"done pretty well" versus "been faithful"	*Forget your spouse: which would you rather be? We strive to be the best in all areas of life—why not spiritually?*
"I will consider you" versus "I will put you"	*There's a world of difference between being considered for a promotion and getting one! Remember, we're talking about rewards from God.*

"a few more" versus "many"	*How exciting to think that God will entrust us with more if we wisely use what we already have!*
"let's ponder" versus "share"	*Sort of like, "I've been thinking about having you over," versus, "Can you come for dinner this Tuesday?" Do you want to share in God's happiness? Do you want to cause some of it?*
"your boss" versus "your master"	*Although it sometimes seems like it, your boss really doesn't own you. And, should you be more concerned about your boss's happiness or your master's?*

Any other observations you'd like to make about this Scripture? Let's read another passage that addresses this issue of doing rather than just thinking. Please turn to James 2:14-26.	**Wait for responses.** **Ask for a volunteer to read or invite someone you know to be a good reader.**

• This is a difficult passage of Scripture—not difficult to understand, but difficult to accept. James does not mince words when he writes, "Can faith without deeds save a man?" (v. 14, paraphrased). "Faith by itself, if not accompanied by action, is dead," (v. 17). In verse 19, James makes it very clear that belief in God alone will not save us. "As the body without the spirit is dead, so faith without deeds is dead" (v. 26).

• Have you ever asked someone about their salvation only to be told, "Oh, I believe in God, and I'm not a bad person"? While we might be eager to share this passage of Scripture with them, we'd better test our own lives against it first!

• Having the faith that God will do what He says seems to be a difficult concept for many Christians. Yet, we actively put our faith in others without a moment's hesitation. We trust our lives to other people every day. Can you name a few?	*Doctors, nurses, paramedics, auto builders and mechanics, bus drivers, airline pilots, the people driving the other vehicles, the pharmacist, the food producer and packager, the electrician, the person who repairs our furnace—who else?*
• You might say that we put our faith in these people because we have no choice—we couldn't live if we didn't trust others. We do have a choice with God— does that make a difference?	**Discuss.**
• But God has never failed us, as people have. God has shown himself throughout history to be loving and faithful. Yes, bad things have happened to good people, but that is because God gave man free will— does that change the fact that God always has our best interests at heart?	**Discuss.**

• These questions are to direct our thinking about whether or not we trust God—have faith in Him. If we do, do our lives prove it? Do our works show it?

Discuss.

Missionary work, preaching, teaching, evangelism, leading the service, leading the music, being in the choir.

• Let's clarify what we mean by "works." Some people think that only "Christian" service counts for God. Can you name some of these types of service?

• But we know that every Christian is a minister of God's Word. Simply by calling ourselves Christian, we become ambassadors for Christ and everything we do or say reflects on Him. We have a responsibility to conduct our lives in a manner that will not bring shame to the name of God. James is very clear about the kind of service he means. He's talking about giving clothes and food to those in need. We certainly don't need a Bible college degree to do that!

We are too busy.
Can busy work keep us from God's work? Are we too busy, or just lazy?
We didn't see opportunity.
Maybe we weren't looking?
I thought someone else would do it.
Hoped someone else would?

• What are some reasons (or excuses!) we give for not serving others?

•Our mistranslated Bible verse came from the end of the parable Jesus told regarding the land owner who left his servants in charge of his property while he went on a journey. Upon his return, he rewarded, and punished, his servants according to what they had done with his property in his absence.

• The meaning of this parable is painfully clear. We are God's servants (His property) and we are living in, and with, and because of His property. He has given each of us portions of His property to care for. How are you doing? Are you using the gifts God gave you to further His kingdom? Will the Master be pleased with your work when He returns?

1. *Start by caring for others—not everybody but somebody.*
2. *We can't do everything, but we can do something.*
3. *Examine our motivations for the things we do that are not meaningful tasks with eternal consequences.*
4. *Actively seek ways to serve. Demonstrate our faith. Be what we say we are. Ask for tasks from the preacher, teacher, mission group, ministry leaders, the person next to us. Serve our next door neighbors.*
5. *Realize that whatever we do is not done to "earn" salvation—just show God that we appreciate His gift.*

•What are some things we can do today to improve our service record?

Discuss.

What's Wrong With This Picture?

Matthew 25:21

"Well thought out, smart and considerate person!

You have done pretty well with a few things;

I will consider you for a few more.

Come, let's ponder your boss's happiness.

What's Wrong With This Picture?

Matthew 25:21

"Well thought out, smart and considerate person!

You have done pretty well with a few things;

I will consider you for a few more.

Come, let's ponder your boss's happiness.

Failure in Success

LUKE 12:13-21

To the students

• On your worksheet there are two diagrams representing two views of the way the world works, or the way things get done. Which diagram do you perceive to represent God's method and which do you perceive to be man's? Why? Let's get some ideas on what the triangles represent.

• First, do you perceive any differences in the way man looks at things compared to the way God does?

• What ideas do these diagrams generate?

For the teacher

Discuss. Be ready for various viewpoints. All have validity.

• The objective of our lesson is to see that God's plan and God's view of success isn't always like man's and, in spite of what we've been taught and what we see in the world around us, God's plan is best in the long run.

• I'd like to suggest this interpretation of the triangles **(if others have already suggested this viewpoint, build on it):**

• The upright triangle represents man's view; the direction of all our efforts is toward one goal or pinnacle of achievement.

• The masses work for (or to be) the one on top. We see examples of this in the military, business, education, etc. Inherent in this view are the concepts of work, struggle, competition, etc.

• The inverted triangle represents God's service to the masses. Christ is the ultimate servant. Many teachers, preachers, and church leaders also understand that their role is to serve.

• What are the differences between these two approaches?

Discuss.

• Which is more natural for us?

Discuss.

• What effect does each view have on selfishness? personal achievement? establishment of priorities? (See Matthew 6:33.)

Discuss.

• Let's turn to Luke 12:13-21 and read the parable of the rich fool.

Ask for a volunteer to read or invite someone you know to be a good reader.

• People often draw some wrong conclusions from this parable. What do you think some of those common misconceptions might be?

Wait for responses before suggesting the following:

1. It is wrong to acquire wealth.

If this were true, how would we explain the many Bible heroes who were rich? Job, Abraham, David, Solomon, Joseph, etc.

2. It is wrong to save for the future

No, this would contradict other verses that tell us to consider the wise ways of the ant (Proverbs 6:6) and count the cost of your plans (Luke 14:28-30).

3. Other

• The conversation right before Jesus began this parable also reveals an interesting misconception. What did the man in verse 13 want from Jesus?

The man wanted Jesus to take his side in a dispute with his brother.

Jesus was not interested in the legality of the inheritance question, but He was interested in the condition of the man's heart!

• And how did Jesus respond?

• Do Christians today ever take the position that it is Jesus' job to solve our problems?

Discuss.
Jesus is interested in changing our hearts; His "job" is salvation.

Now that we've talked about what the parable does not teach, let's talk about what it does teach.

Ask for responses, verse by verse.

---

v. 14 Jesus did not come to solve external problems.
v. 15 Jesus was more concerned about the motives and priorities of man.
v. 15 Ever the teacher, Jesus used this opportunity to teach a life lesson. Words to live by: "A man's life does not consist in the abundance of his possessions."
vv. 16, 17 We can all relate to this situation; it is a question we need to answer.
vv. 18, 19 This is a pretty typical attitude: what's mine is mine to enjoy. The farmer never saw God in his success, never thanked Him.

• How can we avoid this tunnel vision?

See God in all things—Genesis 1:31
Realize that God knows what we need.
—Luke 12:30
Remember that God provides richly.
—1 Timothy 6:17
Realize that we have blessings not because we're special—God gives to all—Matthew 5:48

v. 20 Our perception of our success may not be God's perception.
v. 21 When Jesus said, "This is how it will be," was He necessarily talking about imminent death? **(Get responses.)** We know there are plenty of wealthy Christians alive today; could Jesus be suggesting that those who store up for themselves are not enjoying life as fully as they could? What does it mean to be "rich toward God"?

• What can we do to enjoy our money more fully?

Share, celebrate, praise God!

• So what is the overall message of this parable?

Don't be greedy.

46

• What is greed? Other versions use the word "covetous."

• How can we fight the temptation to be greedy?

Discuss.

1. Spread the wealth! Great joy is found in sharing.
2. Wealth does not give depth to enjoyment. Sometimes a child will set aside a gift and play with the box.
3. True stature comes from within. True joy comes from pleasing God.
4. There is maturity in practicing delayed gratification; invest in the eternal.
5. "A man is rich in proportion to the number of things which he can afford to let alone."
   —Thoreau

CONCLUSIONS

1. God's plan is for us to have and enjoy His creation (material things), but the greater joy is achieved through a relationship with Him. If we believe this, our priorities and life direction will change.
2. Our sense of security or success is often dependent on material things. This can be deceptive since material things are temporary. If our security is in the Lord, however, no one can take it away (Luke 12:33).
3. In the parable the farmer died. Some might ask, "What did he leave behind?" The answer: "EVERYTHING." There are no U-Haul trailers behind the hearse. When we die, we leave what we have and we take what we are. "For where your treasure is, there your heart will be also" (Matthew 6:21). Do we need to rethink our priorities? Let's pray about that.

YOUR HANDOUTS ARE ON THE BACK OF THIS PAGE.
WHEN YOU PHOTOCOPY THEM, DO NOT CUT THIS PAGE APART.

47

Failure In Success

Luke 12:13-21

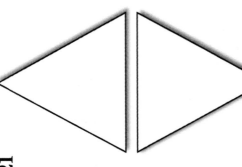

v. 14

v. 15
"A man's life does not consist in the abundance of his possessions."

vv. 16, 17

vv. 18, 19

v. 20

v. 21

Failure In Success

Luke 12:13-21

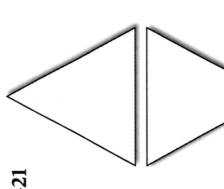

v. 14

v. 15
"A man's life does not consist in the abundance of his possessions."

vv. 16, 17

vv. 18, 19

v. 20

v. 21

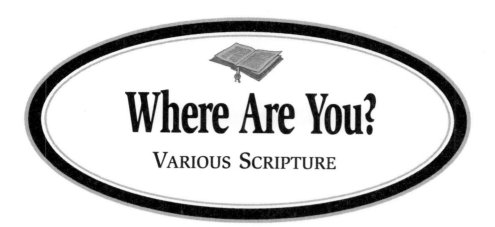

Where Are You?

VARIOUS SCRIPTURE

TO THE STUDENTS

• On your worksheet is a transparent church. To facilitate our thinking and discussion today, please put a mark where you believe you are in the church. Are you coming in or going out? Are you a pew potato? Are you actively involved? Are you near the cross? Go ahead and mark your place.

• Also on your worksheet are three sets of stages of development. How many of the stages can you fill in?

• Our objective in this lesson is to draw closer to God no matter where we are, and to see more clearly what our place in the church might be.
• Let's begin our study by remembering that the church building is only the physical place where the real church meets. What is the real church?

• Looking back at your worksheet, would any of you like to share "where you are?"
• Let's talk about what some of the various locations could mean. Remember, this exercise is just to generate discussion.

FOR THE TEACHER

Distribute student worksheet.

Allow just a short time for thinking and marking.

Allow a short time more.

The body of believers. We are individually and corporately, "the church."

Wait for responses. Discuss locations using material below for ideas.

1. *In the heart of the church:*
   Involved, center of activity, leadership.
2. *At the door:*
   Coming in or going out?
3. *At the window:*
   Trying to see more clearly, or daydreaming?
4. *Near the cross:*
   Trying to be close to Christ
5. *Outside:*
   Considering a commitment, or an just an observer?
6. *In a pew:*
   Participating in worship, or just watching?

• If someone is outside the church with no interest, would they be in our picture?

Not likely.

• Let's examine possible positions a little closer. Who are those closest to the cross?

Those committed to the mission and ministry of the church. Those committed to grow into maturity. Anyone who gives his life in service to God.
Love of God and fellow man.

• Why do they commit this much?

• Who are those in the center, or core of the church?

Those who are committed to supporting the church (verbally and financially).

• Who are those at the door?

Those who realize some need for the church.

• Who are those outside the church?

Those who do not see any need for the church.

• In any growth process there are stages of development. How many were you able to fill in? Anyone fill in all steps? Let's fill them in together.

Don't spend much time on the first two.

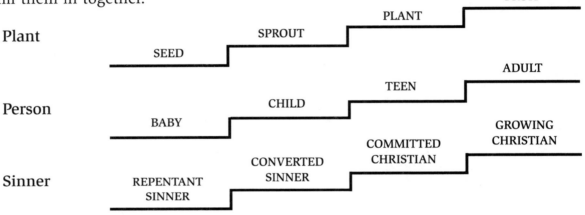

Plant: SEED / SPROUT / PLANT / FRUIT

Person: BABY / CHILD / TEEN / ADULT

Sinner: REPENTANT SINNER / CONVERTED SINNER / COMMITTED CHRISTIAN / GROWING CHRISTIAN

• Let's concentrate on the spiritual steps and check out some Scripture that applies (the texts are interchangeable; evidence of conversion is also evidence of commitment, etc.).

• What is a sinner?

One who disobeys God's will.

• Who is a sinner?

Everyone! Romans 3:23

Step 1   What is repentance?

Turning around—changing attitudes and direction. Acts 2:38; James 4:8-10

Step 2   How are we converted? What is evidence of conversion?

Acts 4:4; 8:34-36; Romans 10:13, 14; Romans 12:1, 2; Galatians 5:16-18; Romans 10:9, 10

Step 3   What is evidence of commitment?

John 3:3-8; Acts 22:16; 2 Corinthians 5:17

Step 4   What is evidence of growth (maturity)?

Matthew 25:37-40; 28:19, 20; Mark 11:25; Acts 2:42-47; 1 Corinthians 11:26; 16:2; 2 Corinthians 9:6, 7; Galatians 6:1, 2, 7, 8; Philippians 3:13-15; 4:6; Colossians 3:2-4; 2 Timothy 2:15, 16; Hebrews 4:16; 1 Peter 3:15; 2 Peter 1:5-8

• Where you placed yourself in the transparent church illustration reflects on where you are in the body of Christ. If you're not happy with your location, you can change it.

• In speaking to his employees, a company president said, "The only way to grow is to change." The statement is deceptively simple. If a plant does not change, it will not grow, and if it does not grow, it will die. We cannot think that our spiritual life is any different.

• If we have not been experiencing spiritual growth, then we must change the way we're doing things. Let's pray about this.

YOUR HANDOUTS ARE ON THE BACK OF THIS PAGE.
WHEN YOU PHOTOCOPY THEM, DO NOT CUT THIS PAGE APART.

51

Where Are You?

Plant

Person

Sinner

Where Are You?

Plant

Person

Sinner

What Time Is It?

GENESIS 21:1-21

To the students

• On your worksheet today is a clock that we are going to use to indicate our emotions. If 12:00 noon to 6:00 PM is a period of joy, and 6:00 PM to 12:00 midnight is a period of sorrow, where are you? Indicate by drawing the hands of the clock, whether your predominate feelings are of joy, or of sorrow.

• What do these expressions mean:
 "Without rain, there would be no rainbows."
 "Without hills, there would be no valleys."
 (And without valleys, we would never have "mountaintop" experiences!)
Discuss.

• The objective of our lesson today is to examine our lives in the light of the Genesis account of Abram and Sarai to see how their emotions were like ours and how their faith may (or may not) be an example for us. Please turn to Genesis 21:1-21. Before we read this together, let me remind you of the events that led up to this part of Abram's story.
• Follow along with me starting with chapter 12. Abram was 75 years old when God asked him to leave his home in Haran and go to a land that God would point out. At this time, God promised to make of Abram "a great nation" (v. 2). When Abram had traveled a far as Shechem, the Lord told him

again, "To your offspring I will give this land" (v. 7). From there he and his clan traveled to Bethel and then toward the Negev desert in the south of Canaan. There they encountered a famine and Abram decide enter Egypt. It was at this point that he instructed Sarai to say she was his sister, so that the Egyptians wouldn't kill him to get her (because Sarai was very beautiful). Pharaoh *did* take her to be one of his wives and the Lord inflicted serious diseases on him and his household because of it. Pharaoh was not too happy with Abram for lying to him, but he returned Sarai to Abram and they returned to the Negev. By this time, Abram's servants, flocks and herds had increased to the point that he was a very wealthy man, but he still had no offspring!
• From the Negev, Abram returned to the place between Bethel and Ai where his tent had been earlier. Lot, Abram's nephew, had been traveling with Abram all this time and together, they owned more flocks and herds than could be supported by one piece of land. At this point, Abram gave Lot his choice of land and Lot chose the plain of the Jordan, which was near Sodom and Gomorrah. After Lot left, the Lord said to Abram, *again,* "All the land that you see I will give to you and your offspring forever. I will make your offspring like the dust of the earth, so that if anyone could count the dust, then your offspring could be counted" (13:15-17).
• Then all the kings of all the surround-

ing city-states and territories starting battling each other, and when Sodom fell, Lot was carried off with the other captives. When Abram heard this, he gathered 318 of his trained men to go rescue him. (This gives you some idea of Abram's enormous wealth—he had at least 318 trained men among his servants!) After Abram's successful raid on the conquering kings—he rescued Lot as well as the other people from Sodom—the other kings allied with him and Melchizedek, king of Salem, pronounced a blessing on Abram. *Once again,* the voice of God came to Abram and said, "Do not be afraid, Abram. I am your shield, your very great reward" (15:1).

• Have you been keeping track? How many times does this make that the Lord promised to make Abram the father of a great nation? (Four.) This time, Abram questioned God. "O Sovereign Lord, what can you give me since I remain childless? . . . You have given me no children; so a servant in my household will be my heir."

• But the Lord replied, "This man [the servant] will not be your heir." He took him outside and said, "Look up at the heavens and count the stars—if indeed you can count them." Then He said to him, "So shall your offspring be" (15:5).
• This makes five times, but this promise was not quite over. This conversation with God was the beginning of the covenant ceremony in which Abram divided the bodies of a heifer, a goat and a ram and arranged them in parallel rows, along with the bodies of a dove and a pigeon. Then Abram fell into a deep sleep and the elements of fire and smoke (representing God) passed between the pieces. It was during this most sacred oath that God told Abram of the four hundred years of slavery that was to come to His people. God finished this covenant with these words, "To your descendants I give this land, from the river of Egypt to the great river, the Euphrates" (v. 18).
• It is after this fifth promise, sealed with the covenant, that we pick up the story today. As we continue to skim through Genesis, use your worksheet to record the emotions stated or implied in each of the players in this heart-wrenching drama. We're going to cover a substantial amount of Scripture, so I will guide you through. You state the emotions of each person as you see them.

16:1 Sarai: doubt, frustration, humiliation, grief
16:2 Sarai: desperation, perhaps anger
16:2 Abram: resignation, doubt, (now 85 years old), tired of wife's nagging?
16:3 Hagar: pride
16:4 Hagar: pride, joy, haughtiness
16:5 Sarai: misery, anger, resentment, jealousy
16:6 Abram: resignation, tired
16:6 Sarai: hated Hagar
16:6 Hagar: hated and feared Sarai
16:7,8 Hagar: terror, desperation
16:9 Hagar: rebellion? fear?
16:10-13 Hagar: new hope, less haughty but probably not humble
16:15 Hagar: great joy
16:15 Abram: joy, pride, trepidation
16:15 Sarai: fierce resentment, fear, anger

17:1-16 Abraham: awe, bewilderment
17:17 Abraham: incredulous (he's now 99)
17:18 Abraham: looked for another way (loved Ishmael)
17:19-21 Abraham: comforted, hope renewed, faith renewed
17:23-27 Abraham: obedient, faith renewed (and in pain!)
18:1-9 Abraham: hospitable, lonely for visitors?
18:9-12 Abraham: knowledge confirmed, probably reassured
18:9-12 Sarah: incredulous, scornful (she was 89 years old!)
18:15 Sarah: afraid
Skip to chapter 21
21:1-8 Abraham & Sarah: indescribable joy!

great relief, honor, happiness
21:1-8 Hagar & Ishmael (now 14): fear, jealousy
21:8 Ishmael: mocking, proud (first born)
21:8 Sarah: fearful for her son
21:11 Abraham: distressed (loved both of his sons)
21:12, 13 Abraham: reassured, probably sorrowful

21:14 Abraham: sad but obedient, relieved? (tension must have been high)
21:14 Hagar & Ishmael: terrified, rejected
21:15, 16 Hagar & Ishmael: thought they were going to die, abandoned
21:17-19 Hagar: hope renewed, extremely grateful to God, refreshed
21:20, 21 Hagar & Ishmael: resentful? poor but proud? determined

• Look at this wide range of human emotion! Isn't it interesting how one set of circumstances can produce such vastly different emotions in individuals depending on their points of view? And how the emotions of one person can fluctuate wildly during the same course of events?

• We may find it tempting to criticize Abram and Sarai for their lack of faith in light of the fact that God promised over and over to provide them an heir. God spoke to Abram personally and through messengers, but He speaks to us through His Word and His Spirit. He has made numerous promises to care and provide for us, but we often conduct our lives as if we alone are in charge. Are any of us in a position to criticize Abram and Sarai?

• What time is it where you are? Are you in a time of joy or a time of sorrow? Or, in some other time?

Encourage students to share.

• Let's look at Ecclesiastes 3:1-8.
• Now look at verses 9-14. Let's read these.

Read it, if you have time.
Ask for a volunteer or invite someone you know to be a good reader.

• What do you get from these verses?
• Time marches on and situations change. How can you find more joy in your situations? (Read James 1:2.)

Discuss.

• Can you think of ways that God has fulfilled promises to you? Keep that question in mind as you review the Scriptures on your worksheet: Psalm 55:22; Isaiah 40:27-31; 1 Corinthians 15:57, 58; John 16:22-24; 1 Corinthians 10:13; Philippians 4:19

Get student responses and supplement with the following:
1. Pray. Ask God to help you understand and cope
2. Believe your prayers will be answered
3. Submit to God's will—don't be stubborn
4. Learn to accept situations
5. Learn how to find humor in adversity
6. Look for the silver lining in every cloud
7. Find ways to put your faith into action
8. Read and reread God's promises
9. Look back at your experiences and see how God has fulfilled His promises to you.

CONCLUSIONS

1. God has made promises to all of us just as He did to Abraham and Sarah. Our job is to discover them and dwell on them.
2. We all go through difficult times in our lives. We should help each other, but most of all trust in God.
3. Seek the help of God and others when we are down.

What Time Is It?
Genesis 21:1-21

Abram ---- Sarai ---- Hagar ---- Ishmael ---- Isaac

Can you think of ways that God has fulfilled promises to you?

Promise

Scripture
Psalm 55:22
Isaiah 40:27-31
1 Corinthians 15:57, 58
John 16:22-24
1 Corinthians 10:13
Philippians 4:19

What Time Is It?
Genesis 21:1-21

Abram ---- Sarai ---- Hagar ---- Ishmael ---- Isaac

Can you think of ways that God has fulfilled promises to you?

Promise

Scripture
Psalm 55:22
Isaiah 40:27-31
1 Corinthians 15:57, 58
John 16:22-24
1 Corinthians 10:13
Philippians 4:19

What Are You Worried About?

MATTHEW 6:23-34; PHILIPPIANS 4:4-8

Don't hand out the worksheets until you make this introductory statement:
Class, I don't want to alarm you but I'm certain there is a thief among us! (Pause for a moment.) Yes, there is a thief in this room. Before you start looking for your wallets, let me assure you that this thief does not take our physical possessions. This thief steals our joy, peace of mind, health, and even life itself.

TO THE STUDENTS
• Can anyone name this thief?

FOR THE TEACHER
Worry.

• We'll use the worksheet today to generate discussion and take notes from the lesson. Take a few minutes to list your concerns.

Distribute student worksheet. Allow about 5 minutes.

• Our objectives will be to examine what causes worry or anxiety, and to find ways to help us overcome it. Let's start by coming up with a definition to put on the board. What is worry?

Wait for responses, then supplement with the following ideas:
Worry is generally unproductive thinking about present circumstances or some future event. Worry involves feelings of anxiety, fretting and stewing, unreasonable concern, fear, dread, agitation, feeling out of control, etc.

• Let's turn to James 1 and read verses 2-8. As we read, look for key words and phrases that reveal how James feels about worry.
• Note especially verse 8. What does the term "double-minded" suggest to you?

Ask for a volunteer to read, or invite someone you know to be a good reader. Discuss the Scripture.

Discuss. *If a person is of a divided mind, he or she is not able to think clearly or assess things in a logical way. Also, it suggests divided loyalty—pulled in two directions, etc.*

• How does worrying over a problem differ from being concerned?
• Why should we *be concerned* but not worry?

Discuss. *Concern prompts us to action— worry does opposite.*
Concern shows a reasonable interest.
Concern is generally open to advice.
Worry often focuses on things that may never happen; "what if . . . ."

Why should we be concerned about our habit of worrying?

1. Worry causes physical problems.

• *During World War II there were 250,000 combat fatalities. In the same period there were 2 million cardiovascular cases—of which 1/3 to 1/2 were due to worry.*

Dr. Charles Mayo has estimated that 1/2 of hospital beds are occupied with people who worried themselves there.

2. Worry interferes with the growth of our faith.

• *It distracts us from appreciating God's gifts and leads us to thinking about, being motivated by, and pursuing riches and earthly pleasures rather than kingdom opportunities. Read Luke 8:14.*

3. Jesus, in the Sermon on the Mount, tells us not to worry.

• *Read Matthew 6:25-34.*

In this sermon, Jesus teaches that we are not to worry because we already know about God's provision. He assumes that His audience (including us!) is fully aware of God's care. Furthermore, He says, "Your heavenly Father knows that you need [these things], so seek first his kingdom and his righteousness." One can almost hear Him say, "What are you worried about?!"

•Besides the evidence of creation, what assurance does God's Word give us? Let's look up the verses listed on your worksheet and fill in the chart.

Scripture	Promises
Isaiah 57:15-19	*God will be with those who are contrite and lowly in spirit, to revive the spirit and the heart. God will not always be angry with us (that would be too much to bear), but He will heal us, guide us and comfort us, causing us to praise Him. He will give us peace.*
Luke 12:22-34	*Luke's account of the Sermon on the Mount gives us another perspective on Jesus' instruction, "Do not worry." The synopsis is: if your priorities are in the right place, you will have no personal needs to worry about.*
Romans 8:26-28	*The presence of the Spirit; assistance from the Spirit; the Spirit prays for us in accordance with God's will (something we don't always know how to do!); no matter what happens God is able and willing to work it out for good—for those who love Him. Amazing, wonderful promises!*
1 Corinthians 10:13	*No temptation is stronger than our ability (given by God) to resist!*
Philippians 4:19	*The KJV reads, "according to his riches in glory by Christ Jesus. This suggests that we are talking about spiritual needs here, and/or that God will supply our physical need as He sees the relation to our spiritual need.*
James 4:2, 3	*God will grant your requests if you ask with the right motives.*
1 Peter 5:7	*God cares for you—He wants to hear your troubles.*

• Is worry a sin?

Discuss.

• How did Jesus answer that question in Matthew 6:25-34?

Worry demonstrates a lack of faith in God, an unwillingness to surrender our needs to God. We'd rather be in charge.

• Since God has promised to take care of our needs and worry says we don't believe Him, is that not accusing God of being a liar?

Perhaps this is the factor that makes worry a sin.

- In verse 26, Jesus asked us to consider the birds. He said God provides for them. Do birds just sit in their nests all day waiting for food?

No, they work hard, beginning early in the morning, to find all the food they need.

- What lesson is there in this for us? Let's consider 2 Thessalonians 3:6-12.

We need to work too. Part of the way God provides for us is in giving us skills and knowledge and the ability to earn money.

- The last item on your worksheet is a formula for overcoming worry. Let's turn to Philippians 4:4-8 and see if we can figure out the formula.

Give students a few minutes to read and think.

Pr + Po + Prr = Pe

Pr: Praise—Rejoice and pray with thanksgiving (Philippians 4:4-6; 1 Thessalonians 5:16-18). The fact that we are instructed to rejoice suggests that it is an act of the will, not necessarily a feeling. "Happiness" is a transitory thing; joy goes much deeper. Happiness is a state of being dependent on outside sources; joy is a chosen attitude.
- Control your feelings.
- Count your blessings (Luke 12:15; Philippians 4:11, 12). It is a fact of life that if you concentrate on what you have, what you don't have loses importance.
- Master altruism, don't expect appreciation.

Po: Poise—Choose faith over anxiety.
Repent of known sin. Check your value system.
Don't retaliate (Matthew 5:44). Removing from ourselves the burden of retaliation give us great freedom!
- Know who you are, your purpose and your hope (2 Corinthians 3:12; Colossians 1:27; Hebrews 6:17-20). Work to be so secure in your knowledge of your worth to God and your purpose for being on earth that you are completely unruffled by false criticism.
- Plan ahead. Don't procrastinate (Proverbs 6:6; Luke 14:28).

Prr: Prayer—Remember the past faithfulness of the Lord (Psalm 31:22; 86:15; James 5:10, 11).
- Communicate with God (1 Thessalonians 5:17).
- Think about the right things.
- Ask for specific help.

Pe: Peace—Absence of anxiety (John 14:27; Romans 15:13; 1 Corinthians 7:15; Philippians 4:6-9).

*Worry, Worry
by Robert Kitchen*

*Oh, worry, worry,
   Fret and stew;
I just don't know,
   What to do!*

*What to do!
   What to do!
I like to worry;
   How about you?*

*Like to worry?
   How can you say
Such a thing
   On this day?*

*When you're in church,
   And it is written:
Don't be anxious,
   Nor worry smitten.*

*Trust in God,
   And His Son.
Have joy;
   Life can be so much fun!*

- Bill Gothard is a traveling evangelist who once gave this definition of worry: "Worry is accepting responsibility that God never intended you to have." Does this pretty well sum up the message of today's lesson?

Discuss.

What Are You Worried About?

List a few of the things troubling you today:

Scripture	Promises
Isaiah 57:15-19	
Luke 12:22-34	
Romans 8:26-28	
1 Corinthians 10:13	
Philippians 4:19	
James 4:2, 3	
1 Peter 5:7	

Formula for Overcoming Worry from Philippians 4:4-8

$$Pr + Po + Prr = Pe$$

Pr

Po

Prr

Pe

What Are You Worried About?

List a few of the things troubling you today:

Scripture	Promises
Isaiah 57:15-19	
Luke 12:22-34	
Romans 8:26-28	
1 Corinthians 10:13	
Philippians 4:19	
James 4:2, 3	
1 Peter 5:7	

Formula for Overcoming Worry from Philippians 4:4-8

$$Pr + Po + Prr = Pe$$

Pr

Po

Prr

Pe

LESSON	ADDITIONAL SCRIPTURE USED
Something to Grow By	Galatians 5; Luke 2:52; 1 Peter 2:1, 2; 2 Peter 3:18; 2 Thessalonians 1:3
Problem? What Problem?	Psalm 20:7; 31; 37:1-7; 62:5-8; 118:8, 9; Matthew 5:21-25; 7:1-5; 6:25-34; 18:15-19; Luke 12:22-29; 21:14; John 14:1; Romans 8:6-8; 15:13; 1 Corinthians 6:18; 10:14; Galatians 3:22; Ephesians 4:25-27; 1 Timothy 6:11; 2 Timothy 2:22; Titus 3:1, 2, 9-11; James 4:7; 12:14-19; 1 John 1:8, 9
What Do You See?	Luke 6:41, 42; Romans 15:1-14; Philippians 2:6-8; James 4:11; 1 Peter 2:12
Hide or Seek?	Psalm 32:8; 73:24; Proverbs 3:5, 6; Romans 12:1, 2; Ephesians 5:8-11; Colossians 1:9; 1 Thessalonians 5:16, 17; James 1:5, 6
You Draw the Line	Daniel 6; Matthew 5:3-12; 6:33; 10:22; Luke 6:22, 23; 18:1; Romans 5:3, 4; 8:18, 28; Galatians 5:16-26; 1 Timothy 3; 2 Timothy 1:8; 3:12; 2 Timothy 2:15; James 2:10. 11; 5:10, 11; 1 Peter 3:14; 4:16; 5:8-10; 2 Peter 3:8, 9; 1 John 3:4, 5:14
What Seed Is This?	Judges 9; Ecclesiastes 11:6; Galatians 6:7, 8
Formula for Success	1 Samuel 17; Hebrews 13:5, 6
What's Wrong With This Picture?	Matthew 25:2; James 2:14-26
Failure In Success	Genesis 1:31; Matthew 5:48; 6:21; Luke 12:13-21, 33; Philippians 4:11, 12; Colossians 3:5; 1 Timothy 6:10, 17
Where Are You?	Matthew 25:37-40; 28:19, 20; Mark 11:25; John 3:3-8; Acts 2:42-47; 4:4; 8:34-36; 22:16; Romans 3:23; 10:9, 10, 13, 14; 12:1, 2; 1 Corinthians 11:26; 16:2; 2 Corinthians 5:17; 9:6, 7; Galatians 5:16-18; 6:1, 2, 7, 8; Philippians 3:13-15; 4:6; Colossians 3:2-4; 2 Timothy 2:15, 16; Hebrews 4:16; 1 Peter 3:15; 2 Peter 1:5-8
What Time Is It?	Genesis 12-18; 21:1-21; Psalm 55:22; Ecclesiastes 3:1-8; Isaiah 40:27-31; John 16:22-24; 1 Corinthians 10:13; 15:57, 58; Philippians 4:19; James 1:8
What Are You Worried About?	Psalm 31:22; 86:15; Proverbs 6:6; Isaiah 57:15-19; Matthew 5:44; 6:23-34; Luke 8:14; 12:15, 22-34; 14:28; John 14:27; Romans 8:26-28; 15:13; 1 Corinthians 7:15; 10:13; 2 Corinthians 3:12; Philippians 4:4-9, 11, 12, 19; Colossians 1:27; 1 Thessalonians 5:16-18; Hebrews 6:17-20; James 4:2, 3; 5:10, 11; 1 Peter 5:7

Record of Use

Lesson Used	Class	Date	Taught By